A DIFFERENT MAGIC

What a Naturalist
Taught a Novelist

by E.M. Beekman

Occasional Papers of Dutch and Flemish Studies
at the University of Michigan at Ann Arbor

DeVries/Vander Kooy Memorial Lecture
delivered on 28 October 1999 by E.M. Beekman

Publication of this book was made possible
by the generous support of Bart Eaton

Printed in China

Mitra Publications Group
527 South Lake Avenue
Suite 102
Pasadena, California 91101 USA

Edited, principal photography, and graphic design
by Greg Asbury, Smith Asbury Inc.

ISBN: 0-9654003-2-8

Library of Congress
Catalog Control Number: 2001116694

FOR DYLAN: *velim haec intellegas et memineris*

Introduction

The literature of the Netherlands attracts far less attention than its renowned art, and the literature of the former colony of the Dutch East Indies, the present Republic of Indonesia, is even less well known. Those who have encountered this literature, which goes back to the end of the sixteenth century, speak of surprising treasures and unforgettable images. One of the indefatigable defenders of this literature in the English language world is Eric Montague Beekman, Multatuli Professor of Dutch Literature, Language and Culture at the University of Massachusetts at Amherst. 'Multatuli' was the pseudonym of Eduard Douwes Dekker, who is arguably the best known of Dutch colonial authors. As editor of the twelve-volume series *Library of the Indies*, E. M. Beekman introduced a new literary experience. His insightful introductions to several volumes as well as his beautiful translations reveal his extraordinary scholarship and have made him an authority on the subject. His latest publications confirm these high standards. There is first *Troubled Pleasures, Dutch Colonial Literature from the East Indies 1600-1950* (Oxford, 1996), which is the first comprehensive examination of Dutch colonial literature in English, and second a translation of *The Ambonese Curiosity Cabinet* by Georgius Everhardus Rumphius (Yale University Press, 1999). The latter is a classic text on tropical marine fauna from the seventeenth century, now made available to the English-speaking world in a scrupulous translation.

The present publication represents a lecture presented at the University of Michigan on 28 October 1999, which links G. E. Rumphius, " the blind seer of Ambon," or the "Indian Pliny," with the fiction of Maria Dermoût, another treasure of Dutch colonial literature. Some years ago many American readers were pleasantly surprised by her extraordinary work, *The Ten Thousand Things*. Beekman points out to us the delicate appreciation of tropical nature that Dermoût learned from Rumphius. She borrowed a large number of details and subtleties from him in order to weave a vision of the natural and supernatural worlds.

The Dutch and Flemish Studies Program at the University of Michigan has grown from a single language course in the 1970s to a series of courses on Dutch and Flemish language, literature, history, and culture. Many students are attracted to courses like "*Anne Frank: Past and Present*" and "*Colonialism and its Aftermath*".

In 1996, the Dutch Studies Program was further enriched by the addition of the De Vries/Vander Kooy Memorial Lecture. Jan de Vries, a Dutch physician with the World Health Organization, who taught at the University of Michigan, and Meindert Vander Kooy, Director of Plant Operations at the same university, were instrumental in the formation of the Netherlands America University League in Ann Arbor. In honor of their extraordinary efforts to promote the study of the language and culture of the Low Countries, the annual De Vries/Vander Kooy Memorial Lecture continues to highlight the Program of Dutch and Flemish studies at the University of Michigan. Previous lectures were given by Richard Lauwaars (1996), Leo Vroman (1997) and Marion Pritchard (1998). In 1999, we continued our memorial in honor of Jan de Vries and Meindert Vander Kooy with the lecture by E. M. Beekman, the first lecture of this series to appear in published form.

This publication would not have been possible without the help of several friends and organizations. My appreciation and gratitude to the author for his enduring dedication, to Bart Eaton for his generous enthusiasm, and to the following organizations for their financial support: the Nederlandse Taalunie in The Hague, the Netherlands, and the Department of Germanic Languages and Literature at the University of Michigan at Ann Arbor.

Ton Broos
Director Dutch and Flemish Studies
University of Michigan at Ann Arbor

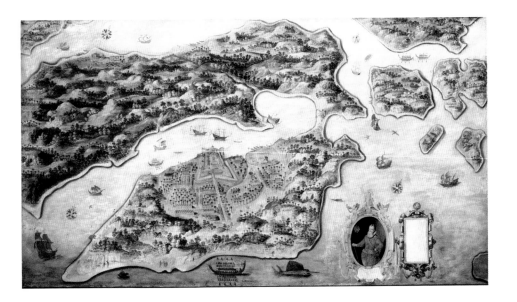

he reader will be introduced to things here that are not common to most of us. The country of their origin is Indonesia, more specifically, the small island of Ambon, 1440 miles east of the capital, Jakarta. They were transmitted to the present time by means of the creative word: two seventeenth-century texts written by a natural historian who was also a poet, and, written by an elderly Dutch lady, one of the most magical novels of the twentieth century. But before examining the unique symbiosis of a man and a woman who lived more than two centuries apart, I will have to inform you, though briefly, about their lives.

Above: From an anonymous painting now in the Rijksmuseum in Amsterdam. The figure is Frederick de Houtman (the first Dutch governor of Ambon). ca1617. Left: The Spice Islands or Moluccas highlighted in a 17th Century map of Asia.

*T*he novel in question is called *De tienduizend dingen* (*The Ten Thousand Things*). It was written by Maria Dermoût and originally published in 1955. A truncated translation was published in New York in 1958 and did very well. The author's maiden name was Maria Ingerman. She was born in 1888 on a sugar plantation in central Java in what were then the colonial Indies. She lived nearly half of her life, or thirty years, in Indonesia. In 1906 she married a jurist, by the name of Isaac Johannes Dermoût, and the couple had two children: a daughter, born on Java, and a son, born on Ambon. They lived for four years on Ambon, the administrative center of the Moluccas (now Maluku province). During her husband's long absences, Maria Dermoût explored the island and its history. She became acquainted with an older woman, Johanna Louisa van Aart, who introduced her to the work of the seventeenthth-century naturalist, Georg Everhard Rumphius.

Because of poor health the Dermoûts were forced to move permanently to Holland in 1933. They lived near Arnhem in order to be closer to their daughter and because of this act of parental piety, they experienced the horrors of the Battle of Arnhem in 1944. After the war ended they discovered that their son had died in a Japanese concentration camp in 1945. Maria's husband died seven years later. By that time she had begun to publish. Her first book, a fictionalized memoir, was published in 1951 when she was 63. She enjoyed her greatest success with *The Ten Thousand Things* after it appeared in 1955. Some of her short stories became anthology pieces in Holland. After enjoying a literary career of exactly one decade, Maria Dermoût died in 1961 at the age of 73, succumbing at almost the same age as Rumphius when he died.

Above: Oil painting by Ina Hooft (1959), of Maria Dermoût. Collection of the Letterkundig Museum in The Hague.

umphius, who was born Georg Everhard Rumpf in Wölfersheim, Hesse (Germany), in 1627, never saw one of his books in print. He entered life in the midst of the Thirty Years War, the worst disaster visited upon Germany before the twentieth century. He enjoyed a fine education for that day and age and had the good fortune that his mother's family was well connected and linked to the prosperous republic of the United Provinces, better known now as the Netherlands.

In 1645, eighteen-year old Rumphius joined a mercenary force that was meant to go to Venice, but after a series of adventures, he found himself stranded in Portugal for almost three years. In 1649, he was back in Germany, but in 1652, he signed on with the VOC or the Dutch East Indies Company, the first multinational corporation of the modern era. He arrived on Java in July of 1653, and that fall sailed for the Moluccas as a soldier in a military campaign. He was stationed on the island of Ambon and never left it for the rest of his life. In 1657, Rumphius switched from the military to the civilian branch of the Company and made rapid promotion during his thirteen years tenure on the coast of Ambon's northern peninsula, Hitu. Sometime during those years he lived with or married a woman called Susanna. We only know about her because he named a lovely variety of terrestrial orchid after her since Rumphius wanted "to commemorate the person who, when alive, was my first Companion and Helpmate in the gathering of herbs and plants, and who was also the first to show me this flower." Rumphius' label has survived the ages for the orchid's modern binomial is *Pecteilis susannae*.

Pecteilis susannae, courtesy of J.B. Comber.

The only confirmed portrait of Rumphius drawn from life. Rumphius' son, Paulus Augustus, drew this portrait of his father sometime between October 1695 and July of 1696 in Kota Ambon. Rumphius was sixty-eight at this time.

D'AMBOINSCHE
RARITEITKAMER,

Behelzende eene BESCHRYVINGE van allerhande
zoo weeke als harde

SCHAALVISSCHEN,

te weeten raare

KRABBEN, KREEFTEN,

en diergelyke Zeedieren,

als mede allerhande

HOORNTJES en SCHULPEN,

die men in d'Amboinsche Zee vindt:

Daar beneven zommige

MINERAALEN, GESTEENTEN,

en foorten van AARDE, die in d'Amboinfche, en zommige omleggende Eilanden gevonden worden.

Verdeelt in drie Boeken,

En met nodige PRINTVERBEELDINGEN, alle naar 't leven getekent, voorzien.

Befchreven door

GEORGIUS EVERHARDUS RUMPHIUS,

van Hanauw, Koopman en Raad in Amboina, mitsgaders Lid in d' *Academiæ Curioforum Naturæ*,
in 't Duitfche Roomfche Ryk opgerecht, onder den naam van

PLINIUS INDICUS.

T'AMSTERDAM,

Gedrukt by FRANÇOIS HALMA, Boekverkoper
in Konftantijn den Grooten.
1 7 0 5.

During these peaceful years on the coast of Hitu, Rumphius
began to work on a natural history of the eastern archipelago.
He collected botanical samples, zoological specimens, and inter-
viewed local peoples for information about the use and dangers
of tropical plants and animals. People brought him things to

buy, he solicited specific items, and cajoled the Company to let him have rare objects. The results of his research were recorded in two classic masterpieces of natural history: his huge herbal, called *Het Amboinsche Kruydboek* (The Ambonese Herbal), and a book on marine fauna and rare animals, entitled *D'Amboinsche Rariteitkamer* (The Ambonese Curiosity Cabinet). Both works were published posthumously.

The second half of Rumphius' life recalls the relentless fate of Greek tragedies. In 1670, this man who cared to render the most insignificant herb or flower in loving detail, became blind 32 years before his death. Four years later, the worst tectonic earthquake that ever hit Ambon killed his wife Susanna and at least one (probably two) of his daughters. In 1687, a fire burned down his house, including his library (if one knows how difficult it was to get books in that part of the world one can understand the magnitude of this disaster), his manuscripts, and the botanical illustrations he had painted himself. What saved him from utter despair was his writing. With incredible stamina and determination, Rumphius kept on working on his monumental texts (the herbal, for example, is 1661 folio pages long), switching from Latin to Dutch so he could dictate his prose to secretaries who were only comfortable in the vernacular.

By 1692, the first six books of the herbal were finished and ready to be shipped to Holland for publication. The governor-general at that time, by the name of Camphuys, was a naturalist himself. Before he released the texts he had a scribe copy the manuscript, then the original was wrapped in oilcloth and put on board the ship *Waterland*. En route to Holland the *Waterland* was attacked by a French squadron (the Dutch Republic was at war with Louis XIV) and sunk.

umphius would not be defeated. During the next decade he corrected and amended the copy which Camphuys had kept. By the end of the century, he finally had the entire herbal finished, in addition to the *Ambonese Curiosity Cabinet*. He finished additional material for his herbal, which constituted a separate volume, only a few months before his death. He died on the 15th of June, 1702, at the age of 74. *The Ambonese Curiosity Cabinet* was published three years after his death, the herbal nearly half a century later.

Dermoût was most familiar with *The Ambonese Curiosity Cabinet*.[1] It is divided into three books or sections. The first one describes crustaceans, jellyfish, sea anemones and an occasional sea snake. Book two became the most famous due to the perennial fascination with shells, a passion that started in the seventeenth century. The book discusses such univalve mollusks as Turbo and Trochus species, opercula of mollusks (an operculum is a plate that develops at the back of the foot of a mollusk and serves to close off the shell after the animal has retracted inside; it was highly prized as an ingredient in making incense and perfumes), and bivalves such as clams, oysters, mussels, and scallops. I should mention that Rumphius did not simply list the shells but was the first to describe the living animals within; that is, he was the first tropical malacologist. The third book was ignored for a long time. But not by Dermoût. It describes local minerals, discusses metals, and reviews a large number of concretions in plants and animals which Indonesians still consider either magical or medical. That last book contains a treasure trove of lore and traditions that is of great interest to a modern ethnographer.

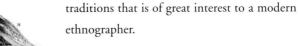

Rumphius, both the man and the work, is the main inspiration
of Dermoût's novel *The Ten Thousand Things.*[2] Readers
understandably assumed that the book's rich details were
autobiographical. In 1958, The *New York Times* reviewer
thought that "unquestionably Maria Dermoût has drawn [the
novel] from her rich memories, which are still as vivid as a coral
garden in clear bay water." But this was not the case. The
individual components of this "great paean of admiration for
the beauty of the world" (as the *Atlantic Monthly* called it) all
derive from Rumphius' *Ambonese Curiosity Cabinet.* The details'
mistaken provenance only emphasizes how poetic and
voluptuous Rumphius' scientific text really is.

I know of no other novel that celebrates a historical figure with
such devotion. Rumphius is present in the novel in three ways:
his books provided Dermoût with the furnishings of the setting,
the historical Rumphius is presented to the reader as if a revered
guest, and he is reincarnated in the person of a Scottish botanist
who is murdered for dumb, blind greed. And mind you,
The Ten Thousand Things is not a historical novel, but rather a
contemporary one that recollects life as lived over five generations.

The
One
Hundred
Things

The novel's plot centers on Felicia, a woman living alone (her husband deserted her) on a plantation on the shore of Ambon Bay. She has learned how to make a living on the greatly diminished property she inherited from her grandmother, a woman of uncommon courage and insight, and one who was more Asian than Dutch. Felicia has only one child, a son, nicknamed Himpies. He is an officer in the colonial army and is killed in an ambush on the neighboring island of Ceram. The novel's occasion or frame is Felicia's annual ritual of commemorating the people who have been murdered the past year on the island, a task almost unbearable that particular All Hollow's Eve because the victims include her murdered son.

'To commemorate' means "to bring to remembrance" and "to make mention of." To make mention of what? Dermoût and Felicia recollect in the Indonesian way; they make mention of the hundred things that pertain to the life of an individual (the ten thousand things express the world at large). Those "hundred things" are "not only the people in his life: that girl, that woman, and that one, this child, that child, your father, your mother, a brother, or sister, the grandparents, a grandchild, a friend, a comrade in arms; or his possessions: your fine house, the porcelain plates hidden in the attic, the swift proa, your sharp knife, an inlaid sword guard from the past, the two small silver rings on your right hand, index finger and thumb, the tame wood dove, your clever black lori; but also: Just listen to the wind roar! — How the whitecaps come rushing in from the open ocean! — The fish are jumping out of the water and are playing with each other — Look how the shells shine on the beaches — and the bay! — the bay! — You will never be able to forget the bay!" (VW, 128).

*View of Ambon's
inner bay. Around
1910. Courtesy of
Het Letterkundig
Museum in the
Hague.*

11

One does not only recall the people themselves but also the "hundred things" that uniquely represented a person. Taken together they become what one might call the furnishings of this novel, its details, the treasured lore of specific lives. The novel's accoutrements are tropical items which gave *The Ten Thousand Things* its exotic cachet.

Photo courtesy
of Bart Eaton.
*Piru Bay, with
the large island of
Ceram in the
distance, as seen
from the watch-
tower of Fort
Amsterdam, in
Hila where
Rumphius was
stationed from
1660 to 1670.*

They include, in no particular order, such things as the egg case of an Argonauta, called the "Linen Coif" by Rumphius, and which he said was held high by the lead dancer during a dance called the Lego Lego (ACC, 94), or the little crabs that were a delicacy to Ambonese ducks who reputedly laid more eggs if they ate the little crustaceans (ACC, 53). The ducks also liked the Summoning Crab, a little crustacean that waves its largest claw as if it is beckoning someone (ACC, 35). With the uncanny perspicacity of the imaginative artist, Dermoût selected the giant clam (its shell was used as a trough for domestic fowl) as an instance of horror. It fits the Rumphian theme, because, as he calls it, the "Beast" within is sightless and was described by Rumphius as "dreadful to behold, because if one looks upon one that is gaping, one sees nothing but a taut skin, full of black, white, yellow, and lead-colored veins, painted like a snake's skin" (ACC, 181). Remember that Rumphius went blind and that the loss of sight is the worst calamity to befall a poet of nature.

Then there are poison plates that warn you of noxious food or drink (ACC, 271), snake stones that draw out venom (ACC, 334), amber in pomanders (ACC, 294), amethysts (ACC, 317), cat's eyes (ACC, 318), varieties of coral (Rumphius believed coral was a marine plant, a notion not dispelled until the second half of the 18th century) with such names as Sea Fan, Sea Net, Coarse Linen, Stag Horn, Sea Rope,[3] black coral that is twisted into arm bracelets,[4] the claws of a variety of crab that were kept as curiosities because they resemble little swans with red beaks (ACC, 23), jellyfish (ACC, 76), sea snails known as Purple Sailors (ACC, 98), and the Coconut Crab which Rumphius likens to "Don Diego" or a Spanish soldier in full armor (ACC, 28).

*R*umphius' shells are ubiquitous in Dermoût's novel. She uses his expressive Dutch nomenclature because those names are memorable poetic metonymies: Red Measles, Night Shells, White Lice, Flea Farts, Cinderellas, Bats, Holsters, and so forth. There are so many Rumphian shells that bear striking names that Dermoût has Felicia concoct a mnemonic story for her son Himpies so he would remember them, a practice once called *een ezelsbruggetje* in Dutch. The two-page story contains the names of 72 shells (VW, 183-5), including the "Podagra Shell" (ACC, 158) — *podagra* meant gout in Latin but Rumphius is thinking of the swollen joints of an arthritic person — and Dermoût's favorite the 'Harpa Amouret,' which Rumphius judged to be "the most beautiful [shell] of its genus, decorated on the outside with broad protruding ribs, which end on top in pointed thorns, and which resemble the strings of a harp, and the little thorns are along the entire curl; the ribs are the color of flesh, the spots between are browner, marked and decorated with white church windows; they are black near the mouth on the belly; the Animal has a great deal of hard and gristly flesh, nicely painted light brown and yellow, with little stars on top." (ACC, 148)

This is a good example of how vivid and precise these seventeenth-century descriptions are. This is poetry because Rumphius tries to capture the quiddity of the animal or plant, and the best poetry has always been concrete and exact. As the German poet Else Lasker-Schüler once put it: a true poet writes 'blue' not 'azure.'

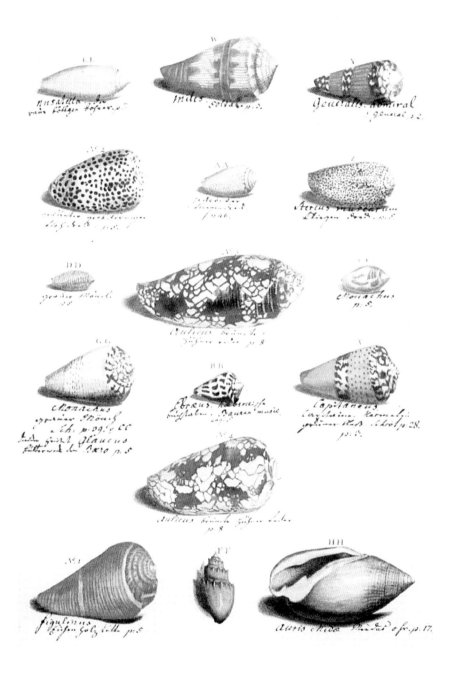

*Plate XLIX from the first (1705) edition of Rumphius' Ambonese Curiosity Cabinet.
This hand colored plate was rendered by Maria Sybilla Merian (1647-1717.*

Ambon from Banda sea

The two most striking images Dermoût borrowed from Rumphius were the "Coral Woman" and the *Kelapa Laut* or "Coconut Palm from the Sea." They required different treatment. The information Rumphius provided in *The Ambonese Curiosity Cabinet* about the coral stone shaped like a woman (ACC, 365) is, except for two details, far more prosaic than Dermoût's amplified creation, while the lore about the fabled palm tree that Rumphius detailed in his Herbal[5] was magical enough that it did not need any further embellishment.

Trees do not grow on the ocean floor. Rumphius was well aware of that, but no one knew until 1769, where some very large and unusual coconuts came from. They were smooth, black, often as large as a foot across, and were found drifting along with the currents in the Indian Ocean. No palm tree was known that could produce such large fruit. In the absence of knowledge, lore proliferated. This is the way Rumphius tells the story.

"The Malay, Chinese, and other Native Seafarers tell us, when talking about its origin and birthplace, that it grows on a tree, far beneath the surface of the sea, similar to a Coconut tree, the top of which can sometimes be seen in silent bays, and around the island of Sumatra, especially in the Bay of Lampon, on Sumatra's southern coast. But then they add something of a fable, because they say that it will vanish, if one looks for this tree, or dives for it.

The Moorish Priests tell an even craftier tale, saying, that there is only one such tree in the world, growing in the abyss of the great South Sea beyond Java, which they call *Segara* or *Laut Kidol*, that is the South Sea, which some maps know erroneously as the Country of *Cidol*.

The tree itself they call *Pausengi*, and its crown sticks out above the water. Its branches are inhabited by the wild Bird *Geruda*, supposedly a Griffin, which flies over these Lands at night, grabbing an Elephant, Tiger, Rhinoceros or other large Beast in its claws and beak, which it then carries to its nest. Currents from every direction are pulled toward this tree, and the Ships that are dragged along by them, must remain there forever, and the people must die of hunger or become prey to the *Geruda*.

This is why the Javanese, and all those who live on the southern coasts of the Great Islands to the East, as far as Timor, do not dare to go further than three miles out, where they'd be out of sight of Land, for if they notice that the current is taking them somewhat further and to the South, they will betake themselves to their rowboat, let their ship drift, and row towards land, for fear they will be pulled to the abyss of Pausengi, wherefrom [sic] no one returns.

And they even insist that some Javanese have experienced this and reported as the truth, that they had been there in their ship and that the Geruda transported them back to Java while they hung on to its Feathers.

They call the fruits of this tree *Boa pausengi* or *Boa sengi*, supposedly the famous *Sea kalappus* which, going against the current, is sometimes tossed onto the beaches of Java and Solor. And they have such a recalcitrant power, that they crawl quite a ways Inland to get to the woods, so that people will not find them, unless they are first discovered by dogs, who will stand and bark at them."

Rumphius did not believe this tale. During his lifetime, it was known that Abel Tasman sailed south of Java between 1642 and 1644 and encountered Australia without being sucked down into an abyss. Yet there remained the physical evidence of these extraordinary coconuts. Like a good empiricist, Rumphius was consumed by the desire to know their provenance, at one point, in a totally different context, expressing his frustration that no one dared to dive for the *Kelapa Laut* that reputedly grew on the bottom of Sumatra's Lampong Bay (ACC, 184).

Tree of Life-from the royal palace archives of Pakubuwono XII, Sultan of Surakarta, Java. Photo by Greg Asbury.

"Pausengi," with which the *Kelapa Laut* is equated, is what Jung would call an archetypal tree. Most civilizations knew of such a Cosmic Tree or Tree of Life. In Norse mythology, there is the well-known tree called Yggdrasil, the familiar biblical Tree of Knowledge, and in Mexico ceramic trees of life are made to this day. The Malay version of such a primordial tree was said to grow on the ocean floor, in a whirlpool known as the "Navel of the Sea."

The Javanese obviously thought it was located south of Java. What Rumphius does not mention is that they believed there was a cavern beneath the roots of the Pausengi tree. It was called *Pusat Tassek* or "Navel of the Sea." A gigantic crab lived in that cavern and when it left its dwelling, the water would rush into the enormous space it had just vacated, a phenomenon that we know as ebb, and when the crab returned, its enormous bulk filled the entire cavern, forcing the waters out, and this we know as flood. The tree, Pausengi, and the crab that lives beneath it are still part of Indonesian wayang or shadow puppet plays.

The bird that sits on one of Pausengi's branches is quite familiar to Indonesians and to India's Hindus. Garuda is the emblem of Indonesia's national airline and is still a deity on Bali because that island retains Hinduism to this very day. Garuda was a mythical creature, half man, half predatory bird. A major figure in India's Hindu pantheon, his story is told in the first book of the *Mahabharata*, he is mentioned in a variety of tales and legends, and he is also fairly common in Indian art. His image has been found in southern India, western India, in Cambodia, on Bali, and on Java in the reliefs of various *candis* (shrines), for instance on Java's Prambanan plain northeast of Yogyakarta. Garuda is the *vahana* (bearer or vehicle) of Visnu, the original Vedic sun god. Addressed as "the warming sun," he was the solar bird. Birds are, in reality and legend, the enemies of snakes — think of Africa's secretary bird, or the eagle of this hemisphere, commemorated in Mexico's national emblem. So too the Garuda is the implacable foe of the *nagas*, usually depicted as hooded cobras. Their enmity symbolizes the ceaseless struggle between the celestial bird and the terrestrial snake. Garuda was popularly said to cure the effect of snakebites, if not of all poisons, which is why the emerald, a stone that in India is considered a talisman against poison, is associated with Visnu's bird. Legends of huge predatory birds are not uncommon. For instance, there is the bird Rukh which Sinbad encountered in his second voyage in the *Arabian Nights*. Marco Polo was told of such a bird living on the island of Madagascar, not to mention the extinct Elephant bird. One wonders if such tales echo a primordial memory of a species of pterodactyl, some of which grew indeed large enough.

Only in 1769, nearly three-quarters of a century after Rumphius' death, did it become known that it was not "Pausengi" that produced those mysterious smooth, black nuts that drifted on the ocean, but that they were the fruit of a real tree. Now labeled *Lodoicea maldivica*, the tree grows only on the Seychelles Islands in the Indian Ocean, some 600 miles northeast of Madagascar. The islands were not known to exist until the seventeenth century, and not really explored until the eighteenth. Perhaps legends were in order, because these palm trees and their fruit are natural prodigies. The tree grows very tall; the average is fifty feet and a height of one hundred feet is not uncommon. It also grows very straight, which is quite unusual for a coconut palm. The tree will not flower until its thirtieth year and it takes another decade for the flower to turn into a ripe fruit. The flowers come from huge spadices or fleshy flower-spikes. The way the Mexican poet, Octavio Paz, describes it, the male spadix is "shaped like a phallus, measures three feet in length, and smells like a rat."[6]

When this palm finally produces fruit they are the largest of the palmae. Each nut weighs about forty pounds and they grow usually in clusters of four or five. Each one is about eighteen inches long and wide, heart-shaped, and large enough that it was often used as a container because it can hold three to four gallons of water. After the seeds have germinated, it is the empty fruits, usually two-lobed and surrounded by a fibrous husk, that are found drifting on the open ocean. Known as *coco-de-mer*, these floating mysteries were found for centuries by travelers who ascribed great powers to them. They were considered a most excellent antidote against all venom. One can well imagine that Dermoût did not need to add much to this material. She only intimated the fact that Rumphius never saw the real tree and never knew of the existence of the Seychelles Islands.

The Coral Woman is somewhat different. Rumphius relates the tale quite soberly. In 1681, he tells us, a coral rock was hauled from Ambon Bay that had the shape of a woman. Local people believed it to be the petrified body of a Javanese woman who had fallen overboard several hundred years before. The men who brought the chunk of coral to land insisted that when they pulled it out, the coral rock sighed. Rumphius bought the rock for one rixdollar and put it in his garden. Later he stuffed seeds in the pitted coral stone and the seeds took, so that, as he reports, "there grew various small plants and flowers from the selfsame body" (ACC, 365). Dermoût amplified these few givens into an original creation, a woman whose nakedness is covered by the tiny plants and flowers Rumphius seeded and who, because she came from the bottom of the sea, might well

Photo of the Coral Gardens in the Indian Ocean or South Sea.
Photo by Greg Asbury.

22

have privileged knowledge of the *Kelapa Laut*. Dermoût makes Felicia wonder if Rumphius "ever stood near her and looked at her with his nearly sightless eyes, in the evening when it was still and dark, and light beneath the stars, and did he ask her if ..." (VW, 131). Did he ask her if she had seen Pausengi when she was down below because he "was dying to see the Cocopalm of the Sea — black or purple or a pinkish red (with the Crab and the Bird) in the deep blue and green water of the inner bay — just once, before he became totally blind, and that would not be long now? And what did the coral woman, what did the closed coral mouth answer him?" (VW, 132).

And in the novel's apotheosis, Dermoût brings all the things I mentioned, along with all the characters, brings them all back in one overwhelming tableau: "The purple Coconut Palm of the Sea and beneath it stood her [Felicia's] grandmother and Mr. Rumphius and the coral woman in her dress of flowers; her grandmother held the poison plate from Ceram and she put the 'little sentinels of Happiness' in it which she had plucked from the trunk of the Tree; between the roots of the Tree sat the crab, 'Don Diego in full armor,' and he ruled ebb and flood and the holy Bird had its nest in the branches up above" (VW, 296).

All the shells are there, the people too, both real and imagined, and Felicia for one brief, moonlit moment *sees* that this magical multitude is connected but not in a willful way. All that was "far more than the hundred things, and not only hers, a hundred times 'a hundred things,' next to each other, separate from each other, touching one another, sometimes flowing into one another, without any real bonds anywhere, and yet forever linked to each other" (VW, 297).

*E*verything I mentioned, and much more besides, derives from Rumphius' *Ambonese Curiosity Cabinet.* That seventeenth-century text is more than what the intellectual buzzword 'subtext' connotes, for Dermoût used it to nourish her fiction the way a growing plant partakes of a rich and cultivated soil. It seems to me to be a rare instance of a true artistic symbiosis, a mental and emotional conjoining that is intimate and mutually beneficial. This association had even a moral benefit.

Perhaps it is clear by now that Rumphian generosity disdains materialism. It is a natural affluence you can acquire just like that, by chance, gratis, for nothing. There is no stock index for these assets, because they can be shared by everybody, and their relative value is a personal matter. The Indonesians call these assets *pusaka.*

Recalling "the one hundred things" of another's life. (opposite, photo illustration by Greg Asbury)

Pusaka– Pusaka ⸭

*P*usaka is an Indonesian noun usually translated as 'heirloom.' That is not good enough. Pusaka pusaka* [*Bahasa Indonesia does not know a plural form, you simply repeat the singular or write '2' above the noun] are more often than not ascribed magical properties, and an economic value does not determine what object is raised to the status of pusaka. For instance, a pebble can be a pusaka but a credit card cannot. Pusaka² have their proper soul and significance. Each object has, as Dermoût noted, "its own history, its own life, like [that of] the living people they temporarily belonged to."⁷ The non-western, non-economic notion of pusaka is very well captured by Roland Barthes when he tried to convey what Japanese poetry dealt with: "the apprehension of the thing as event and not as substance."⁸

This partakes of the core of *The Ten Thousand Things* as well. The magnificent grandmother who raised Felicia owned some jewelry, like any other lady of a certain social status. What the grandmother calls her "treasure" consists of an ordinary looking plate and two small wooden boxes, both containing what seem plain pebbles (VW, 142).

The first box contains a snake stone, the other a *chamites* or a stone that gives birth to its own kind. Dermoût found all three in Rumphius' *Ambonese Curiosity Cabinet*. The grandmother's snake stone is a medicinal stone. If you have been bitten by a venomous animal, you place this stone on the wound and it will stick to it like a leech. When it has drawn out all the poison it will fall off by itself, just like a satiated leech. Rumphius called it the "Ceylonese Snake Stone" and noted that if one wanted to recharge the stone's powers one should place it in a dish of cow's milk but preferably in the milk of a nursing woman. The milk will draw the poison out of the stone and turn blue (ACC, 339).

There are a number of different snake stones. What was called "the natural one" was obtained by hanging a water snake by its tail over a pot of water in such a way that it could just reach the water surface with its tongue. After a few days of hanging like that, the snake will spit the stone out and you will know that it has done so because all the water in the pot will have dried up (ACC, 339). The ethnic Chinese of Rumphius' day obtained another stone from what seems to have been a most accommodating reptile. This snake would remove the stone from its head when it needed to eat or drink, and that gave a person the opportunity to steal it (ACC, 341).

The grandmother kept the birthing stone for sheer magic, but the poison dish had a practical application. It will warn of the presence of poison in anything that is placed on it by making a crackling sound. These *pingan batu* were first brought to the archipelago, according to Rumphius, by the legendary Chinese admiral Sampo (ACC, 274). The grandmother's special drawer which harbored these three priceless treasures also contained some mollusks that acted as their guards. According to the Papuas, the animals that live in these shells can go without food for an entire year, and they used to put them with their personal belongings. If one of the animals died before its appointed time the local people believed that something had been stolen from them (ACC, 107). The grandmother insists that her treasure is protected by these sentinels and makes sure there is the requisite changing of the guard. "As long as the treasure was guarded by the living sentinels, no thief would dare touch it, and as long as the treasure was in the drawer, the house on the Kleyntjes plantation would be preserved from misfortune, disease, poverty, and from Fenom, and other unmentionable things. . ." (VW, 144). These invaluable shellfish, which she calls "the sentinels of happiness," also derive from Rumphius (ACC, 107).

66 *...pusaka...* **can never be bought from someone...99**

There is one other important thing about these pusaka pusaka that should be mentioned. And it is very anti-Western. These treasured items can never be bought from someone; you should either find them yourself or they should be given to you, just like that, gratis, for nothing.[9] A gift, be it from nature or from a friend, cannot be bought with money. In fact, to invoke the economic prerogative is an insult and lethal to the magic of the object. The grandmother knows this fundamental rule very well. She despises money, because money tries to disguise the fact that life's basic commodities are gifts. One day, the grandmother becomes outraged when Felicia suggests that they sell produce to make a living. "What do you mean," the older woman exploded, "sell! For money? We! You can't mean that, we didn't pay any money for it. The animals give us milk and eggs, the garden gives us fruits and vegetables, mussels come from the bay; the black coral I need for bracelets I get from the coral divers because I give them medicine when they're sick; the only thing is sugar, white sugar for making preserves, you can't use palm sugar for that" (VW, 162). Rumphius shares this sentiment as well. Speaking of a magic bracelet that fell from the sky, Rumphius informs his readers that he completely agreed with the local population when they maintained that a

pusaka loses its magical powers after it has been sold to some-
body; and they say this "of all Curiosities which one has not
found oneself or that were not given as a gift, but were bought
with money" (ACC, 279). He repeats this injunction several
times in his work and other comments make it clear that he was
irritated by and critical of European greed and covetousness.

I do not know if this conviction is still as strong in modern
Indonesia, a society as corrupt as any other that is controlled by
global conglomerates, but Rumphius is witness that it was still
true in the seventeenth century. Dermoût ruefully understood
that it was quixotic in the twentieth century. By the way,
Rumphius also fell victim to the pressures of business practices
when his bosses forced him to sell his curiosity collection of
360 items to the last Grand Duke of Tuscany, Cosimo III
(ACC, 233). Cosimo happened to be a particularly reprehensible
aristocrat, but he was a prospective customer of the Dutch East
Indies Company. Rumphius refers to 1682, the year he was
forced to ship his cherished collection to Europe, twice as often
as the year he became blind or the year his wife and child died
in the earthquake.

he world shared by Rumphius and Dermoût is sane and sensible but it is not a scientific one ruled by Cartesian presumption. To be sure, Rumphius was not persuaded that everything his informants told him was true, but he never denigrated them because, he felt almost anything he heard had a modicum of truth. Dermoût has no need for caveats because fiction presumes anything to be true, at least as long as the duration of the telling. But both would advocate that you do not dismiss this lore as false because within the context it is encountered it is viable and right. It has a logic of its own, a view of the world shared by pre-modern Europe. The grandmother's drawer provides an example. Note that the greatest treasures are antidotes to poison or Venom, which both Rumphius and Dermoût consistently spell with an 'F'. The poison dish will warn you if your food or drink has been tampered with, and the snake stone will cure the effect of a venomous bite. How?

The answer is homeopathy, a theory that has never gone out of fashion. The principle is embedded in the original Greek compound. The noun is a combination of *homos* which means 'the same' and *pathos* which means 'suffering.' A homeopathic cure makes you suffer (at a manageable level, of course) the same symptoms as the full-blown disease, with the hope that this will boost your immunity to it. Homeopathy is the principle of flu shots or tetanus shots. The snake stone operates on the same principle. The reasoning is that, if such a concentration is found in the head of a snake, it follows that it should be efficacious against the venomous bite of reptiles. We know of course that this is not the case, but we are also aware that today's antidotes to snakebites are manufactured from the specific poison of a species.

Indonesian people believed (and still do) in the magical powers of stony concretions found in animals and plants. Properly speaking, as Rumphius instructs us, one should distinguish between the *mestika* (or magical fetish) and the *guliga* (or medicinal stone). The distinction is not rigidly maintained and the two often overlap. Say that the well-known bezoar and the snake stone are *guliga*, and that the birthing stone and the chamites (a concretion found in certain mollusks) are magical *mestika*. *Mestika* are produced by humans, pigs, deer, cats, insects, lizards, birds, fishes, mollusks, trees, flowers and fruits. Rumphius described them with fascinating detail in the third book of his *Ambonese Curiosity Cabinet* (chs. 46 to 75), and the pages he devoted to them are our only detailed source on these stones and their use.

Most of these stones were considered antidotes to poison. Even a cursory examination of Rumphius' work will disclose a bewildering number of supposed cures against all manner of toxins. There is the common snakebite. Snakes are everywhere in Indonesia. In the rainy season you check between your sheets before you go to bed, you better watch where you walk in the grass, and they can suddenly appear at eye-level in shrubs and small trees. But there are also poisonous fish, poisonous mollusks, poisonous crabs (the ones with black claws are toxic), poisonous fruits, leaves and roots. Seeds can poison you (also known as getting high), spines of sea urchins can infect you, the odor of certain flowers can sicken you, and jellyfish can sting you. Rumphius' world is a most toxic environment and everywhere is the threat of a baneful infliction.

o make matters worse, your own kind will try to poison you, both literally and figuratively. By the latter, I mean the consequences of an evil spell. Rumphius noted that every smart Indonesian once carried an anti-poison and anti-enchantment kit with him wherever he went, containing two kinds of shells, three or four kinds of coral all of which, after being crushed and taken with some water "is a proven Antidote against all sorts of ingested poison, and it will kill its powers...furthermore, it can also be used against particular enchantments or villainies, which they love to inflict on each other, taking someone's manly powers away; which is why they always have these things ready, when they travel far from home..." (ACC, 178).

From one perspective, Rumphius' classic texts seem like one huge handbook on toxins and their antidotes. Dermoût perpetuated this obsessive reality but she also gave it a larger dimension. The grandmother tells Felicia that "wherever people are you'll find at the same time misfortune, sorrow, wickedness, sometimes even venom — you know, Fenom — but that doesn't mean that we are cursed..." (VW, 171).

What the grandmother knows, and what Felicia will only learn to accept at the end of the novel, is the inevitability of life's misfortunes and sorrows. Those are natural conditions, a fact of life that the spinmasters of the American entertainment industry refuse to acknowledge. This is not sentimentality. Neither Rumphius nor Dermoût was ever sentimental. They were both capable of great feeling and exhibited a tender affection for even the most insignificant denizen of nature's realm. But they did not suffer from the sentimentalist's curse of viewing life as a choice between only two possibilities and then denying the existence of the negative one. That is to say, an animal is either Bambi or a cockroach, ignoring the necessity of Bambi's father rutting in the fall, or that cockroaches only infiltrate our space when civilized behavior has fled.

Rumphius, Dermoût, and the grandmother were no such fools. They know and accept that diseases kill, that aged parents die, that fate can cause financial ruin. But they clearly put 'Fenom' on a different level. What is it? It is impossible to give a single, inclusive definition, but you will know it when you have the misfortune of encountering it. It is *not* part of nature; it is a human curse. Perhaps one could call it radical evil or man's inhumanity to man. Obvious examples are the Second World War, or Milosevic's expulsion of Albanians from Kosovo. A more bizarre instance are the thousands of Indian and Pakistani troops who have been fighting each other for the past fifteen years for the possession of a glacier in the Western Himalayas. A more pertinent example for the present context is the city of Ambon, known as Kota Ambon (to distinguish it from Pulau Ambon, or the island), 1440 miles east of Jakarta, Indonesia's capital. This is the town where Rumphius lived for thirty two years and where his house burned down in 1687. That calamity was due to misfortune. Nor was it Fenom that caused the terrible tectonic earthquake on Chinese New Year in 1674, the disaster that killed his wife and child. That was a natural event and it must be endured. But the destruction in Kota Ambon in 1999 was caused by Fenom. 3,000 homes have been burned down. At least 6,000 people have been killed. Three hundred thousand residents have fled and live in squalor elsewhere.[10] And for what reason? It started in January of 1999, when a Christian bus driver had an altercation with a young Muslim. The sectarian violence escalated into a full-blown holy war.

"Holy war" is an oxymoron, for no war can ever be holy. The absurdity of killing people for their religious beliefs is illustrated by an Ambonese man who, while getting his homemade shotgun ready, told a reporter: "If you die, you die in the name of Christ, if you kill a man, you kill him in the name of Christ."[11] A Muslim would phrase it the same way, he would only substitute Allah for Christ. This kind of situation is sheer madness. A commentator in Jakarta correctly warned that there is no solution to this crisis. The reason she gave was that "the atmosphere is too poisoned now."[12] That is what Dermoût meant by 'Fenom.' A people so infected with hatred that they will make weapons out of anything. One report describes a shotgun that had ordinary batteries strapped to the stock. The batteries were supposed to ignite the charge, which was a mixture of old-fashioned gunpowder and sulphur, the latter obtained from pulverized match heads. It fired scraps of metal. Bows and arrows also did service, as did slingshots (the sling fashioned from an inner tube), or spears cut from aluminum pipes and, of course, the ever-present *parang* or machete.[13] When you hear of such weapons and the killing frenzy that ordered them, you realize with horror that not much has changed since Rumphius' day. You become despondent when you hear of villages razed to the ground, villages that are frequently mentioned in Rumphius' work, such as Hative Besar, Passo or Hila. And this madness is not over yet, not by a long shot.

I just said that you become 'despondent' when confronted with this evil that infects people and that courses through their veins like a toxic madness. But Dermoût, via the grandmother in her novel, tries to teach us that one should not remain despondent but turn defiant. There is no cure for this kind of poison, no simple solution that will eradicate this evil and its consequences.

But we should not let it intimidate us, scare us, or break us. "We should," the grandmother teaches Felicia, "we should try to remain proud people, stand tall" (VW, 171). Is there then no antidote, no counter force? Dermoût intimates that there is, but it is a simple, subdued, and undramatic one. The inspiration comes once again from Rumphius who now turns out to be even more than a poet of nature: he is a moral standard. The remedy is a peculiarly Asian aid for living, because it is connected to the pusaka. The answer is embedded in the novel's section entitled "The Professor," a superb piece of writing that once again was inspired by the work and the life of Rumphius.

"...we should try to remain proud people, stand tall..."

35

*U*nless the reader is well acquainted with Rumphius' *Ambonese Curiosity Cabinet*, he or she will never know how profoundly Dermoût plumbed Rumphius' work. And hardly anyone ever knew that the details of the professor's story are also inextricably connected with Rumphius' legacy.

The surface tale is very simple and quickly told. A Scottish professor, by the name of McNeill, comes to the Indies to do field work for a new standard text on the region's botany based on Rumphius' *Herbal*. The Botanical Garden in Bogor on Java recommended that he take an assistant along, a young Javanese nobleman by the name of Raden Mas Suprapto. When they arrive on Ambon, the professor and his assistant go on field trips trying to get local children to bring the professor botanical specimens for which he pays with shiny, freshly minted coins. One day, he gives a small girl two shiny quarters for a bunch of orchids. She is a member of a community of migrant workers. Some of the men notice the professor's largesse and decide that he is rich and carries a lot of money on him. One afternoon, when the Javanese assistant is deathly ill with malaria, the professor goes off on his own and the migrants kill him for the change he has in his pocket. They wrap his corpse in an old mat, weigh it down with rocks, and toss it overboard in Ambon's inner bay. The four men who killed him are apprehended and punished.

The professor's senseless murder, motivated by petty greed, a minor but no less lethal version of Fenom, are based on real events. It starts with Elmer Drew Merrill (1876-1956) once one of America's foremost tropical botanists. Once called the "American Linnaeus," Merrill's specialty was tropical botany and he published more than 500 scientific papers and books on the subject. He worked at the Bureau of Science in Manila from

1902 to 1923. During his tenure there he sent an associate to Ambon to collect the plants that Rumphius described in his voluminous *Herbal.* The younger botanist was Charles Budd Robinson, born in Nova Scotia in 1871. With him went a Javanese assistant from the Botanical Garden in Bogor by the name of Mardjuki. Robinson arrived on Ambon in July of 1913 and began his field work. Within a few months he was found murdered. It seems that a local superstition and a linguistic confusion were the causes of his pointless death.

His killers were emigrant workers from Buton, an island off Celebes (now Sulawesi), who were living in a settlement about nine miles outside the capital, Kota Ambon. At the heart of the tragedy are two words which sound very much alike: *kelapa,* which was mentioned before and which means 'coconut' in Malay, and *kepala*, which means 'head.' Several regions in Indonesia honored ritual headhunting. One of these was Ceram, the large island that hovers over diminutive Ambon. The Alfurs on that island called this activity *potong kepala*. *Potong* means 'to cut' or 'to chop,' so the phrase means "to chop someone's head off." In an ethnographic article about Ambon published in 1941, but based on observations from the 1930s, a Dutch ethnographer wrote that even at that time people still "believed strongly in 'potong kepala' and were deathly afraid of what they said were creatures roaming around during the season of cloves[14] looking to decapitate people."[15] The story goes that Robinson yelled at someone up in a coconut palm to cut down a coconut for him (*potong kelapa*) and by mistake said *potong kepala* (cut your head off), and that the local people attacked and killed him with ax blows.[16] You can tell that Dermoût kept the general outlines of this tragic event, but ignored the linguistic confusion.

The detail of paying for botanical samples with shiny new coins derives from another American scientist, the zoologist A. A. Bickmore (1839-1914), who traveled all the way to eastern Indonesia for the sole purpose of finding the shellfish Rumphius had described in the second book of his *Ambonese Curiosity Cabinet.* He traveled with a copy of the folio-sized book (i.e. 17 1/2 inches long and 10 1/2 inches wide) and showed the illustrations to local people so they could tell him where he could find the shells. If he had known Dutch, he would have found all he needed in the text. Rumphius' information is so precise that a Dutch expedition, that went to Ambon in 1990 to do the same thing as Bickmore had done, discovered that Rumphius' directions were perfect. Bickmore states that he always traveled with "shining coin," as he put it, which he was always "careful to display to their gloating eyes." "To give the trade more éclat," Bickmore wrote, "I took a good quantity of small copper coins and distributed them freely among the small children as I passed along. The result of this manoeuvre was most magical; everybody was anxious to make my acquaintance and sell me shells."[17]

Dermoût combined these details and events and reinvented them to fit her theme of life's inexplicable connections and the fearful consequences of the Fenom that infects people. The Fenom that killed the professor was greed and it was vile. For as the police officer states: the local people were disgusted that four young men armed with machetes crept up on a defenseless and myopic old man and cut him down for a handful of change (VW, 281). But the professor had bested his killers even before his needless death. He had done so by means of Rumphius.

One evening, on board the pacquet boat, the professor talks to his Javanese assistant about Rumphius' *Ambonese Curiosity Cabinet.* Dermoût makes him single out two texts: one describes a jellyfish, known as the Portuguese man-of-war, which Rumphius called "mizzen" because it resembled the triangular aft-sails of his day (ACC, 77-8), and the other is a brief but beautiful text about what he thought was another jellyfish but which in reality is a pelagic snail, these days popularly known as the Purple Sailor (ACC, 98). Dermoût has the professor read the following sentences from Rumphius' descriptions- first from the description of the snail, a creature Rumphius called a Gelly-Boat. "It has a single shell, thin and transparent; at the bottom a light violet blue veering to the color of lead on top; the mouth is wide, round, but it has a little corner at the bottom that sticks out like a Flew or hanging lip, and they are white inside. This little Sea-Gelly is perfectly clear, like a small crystal with a blue sheen, and it consists of nothing but slime. The little boat laid there with the opening up, and the little Sea-Gelly stood upright like a small pillar, appearing to sail with a faint breeze." When his assistant does not react, the professor next quotes some sentences from Rumphius' description of the jellyfish he called the 'mizzen': "At its back are many little fleeces sideways, broad on the bottom, fastened onto the back, on top forming a point, similar to a half-sail, called a mizzen. All these little sails are at the top joined by a seam running across, which allows it to lower and raise these sails when it feels a wind and wants to sail. The body is of a transparent color, as if it were a crystal bottle filled with that green and blue Aqua Fort. The little sails are as white as crystal, and the upper seam shows some purple or violet, beautiful to see, as if the entire Animal were a precious jewel" (ACC, 77-8).

It does not matter that Dermoût rearranged the sequence of the sentences in the two totally separate texts. Her poetic instinct was infallible, for the point she wants to make is contained in a sentence from the description of the pelagic snail, a statement of fact that acquires even more resonance after the beauty of the creatures has been lodged in the reader's mind. The sentence is: "Wondrous to see such a fleet of easily a thousand little ships sail so agreeably together."

The point, as the professor tries to tell his assistant, is that when "Rumphius dictated this, he was blind, blind as a bat, my friend; his wife and daughter crushed under a collapsing wall during an earthquake, his house that burned down later on, burned to the ground with everything in it, all the work of a lifetime, except for a few hundred pages, all his drawings, and then he can write 'such a fleet of easily a thousand little sails, wondrous to behold.' It makes us, you and me, such ungrateful dogs" (VW, 264).

Fort Belgica on Banda Neira. Gunung Api (fire mountain) is in the background. (Photo courtesy of Bart Eaton).

Restored Fort Amsterdam on the Hitu peninsula, Ambon, in the town of Hila. Rumphius was posted here (1660 to 1670) early in his career with the Dutch East Indies Company (VOC). (Photo courtesy of Bart Eaton).

Rumphius is finally recognized as the master, the *guru*. Although I hesitate to use that word, since it has been degraded in the Western world, it befits an Asian context. What he teaches is that we should see beauty even if one's life is a disaster, even if malignity rears up and strikes. In other words, we should try to transcend the now, overcome the constrictions that society and the human condition have forced upon our souls. Rumphius' work had a material side to it: he always tried to find medicinal benefits in plants or animals. And yet the jellyfish has no material value, is useless to apothecaries. But Rumphius saw the beauty of the animal and, as Schopenhauer (1788-1860) wrote a century and a half later, things will increase in beauty when we are conscious only of them and not of ourselves. The pure objectivity of perception can make us happy.[18] Here we have the connection with the notion of pusaka, for the beauty of a jellyfish is free, gratis, for nothing, it is literally priceless. That is a great benefit, for life is always difficult, but one should be able to warm one's soul in the glow of beauty, as Felicia does at the end of *Ten Thousand Things*.

Gunung Api across the bay from Banda Neira. This is one of many active volcanoes in the "ring of fire" that comprises the Indonesian archipelago.

umphius' text was nature. He came to understand that, in the words of the twelfth century mystic Hugh of St. Victor, "all nature is pregnant with sense, and nothing in all of the universe is sterile."[19] By concentrating on finding that sense, Rumphius managed to overcome a life which knew almost as many afflictions as Job. His research culminated in two classic masterpieces of natural history, his huge tropical *Herbal* and the *Ambonese Curiosity Cabinet,* a book detailing the animals of tropic seas. Maria Dermoût read those books and understood the man who wrote them. The conjunction of the twentieth-century novelist and the seventeenth-century poetic scientist became a mutually beneficial relationship.

What Dermoût gleaned from Rumphius and what she conveyed to her readers via her fictional character Felicia, is that wisdom is not only in the heart but also in the object. It requires listening. We should listen to nature as Rumphius did. It is a gift, because it is free, gratis, for nothing. It will restore us and it can provide solace. And that is why it is magic.

NOTES

1. All references are to the English edition. Georgius Everardus Rumphius, *The Ambonese Curiosity Cabinet*. Translated, edited, annotated, and with an introduction by E. M. Beekman. New Haven: Yale University Press, 1999. All subsequent references to this edition are provided in the text with the abbreviation ACC, plus page number.

2. All references are to the comprehensive edition of her collected work in one volume, Maria Dermoût, *Verzameld Werk*. Amsterdam: Querido, 1984. References given in the text with the abbreviation VW and page number. All translations are the author's.

3. Rumphius discussed coral in his *Herbal*, Book 12, in vol. 6: pp. 193-256.

4. Vol. 6: p. 199.

5. In ch. 8 of bk. 12; vol. 6: pp. 210-217.

6. Octavio Paz, *The Monkey Grammarian* [1974]. Transl. Helen R. Lane. (New York: Seaver Books, 1981), p. 46.

7. Quoted in Johan van der Woude, *Maria Dermoût. De vrouw en de schrijfster* (Den Haag: Nijgh & Van Ditmar, 1973), p. 195.

8. Roland Barthes, *L'Empire des signes* (Geneva: Skira, 1970), p. 101.

9. "Zo maar cadeau present voor niets om te houden;" VW, 143.

10. Figures provided by J. L. Nanere, Chancellor of Pattimura University on Ambon, in an interview: *NRC-Handelsblad* (Weekeditie), 12 October 1999.

11. Reuters dispatch of 8 March 1999.

12. Dispatch by Vaudine England from Jakarta, printed in the *South China Morning Post*, 10 March 1999.

13. Reuters dispatch of 8 March 1999.

14. The months of November and December.

15. H. J. Jansen, "Ethnographische bijzonderheden van enkele Ambonsche negorijen (ca. 1930)", *Bijdragen tot de Taal-, Land-, en Volkenkunde van Nederlandsch-Indië* (1941), 98:3, p. 337.

16. E. D. Merrill, "Charles Budd Robinson, Jr.," *Philippine Journal of Science* (1914) 9:191-197.

17.   Albert S. Bickmore, *Travels in the East Indian Archipelago*
       (New York: Appleton, 1869), pp. 134, 174.

18.   "Demnach wird das Bewußtseyn anderer Dinge, also die anschauende
       Erkenntniß, um so vollkommener, d.h. um so objektiver, je weniger wir uns
       dabei des eigenen Selbst bewußt sind." This is from ch. 30 in the second part
       of *Die Welt als Wille und Vorstellung*, "Ergänzungen zum dritten Buch." the
       author quotes from: Arthur Schopenhauer *Die Welt als Wille und Vorstellung*,
       4 vols. (Zürich: Diogenes Verlag, 1977), II, 2:436.

19.   "Omnis natura rationem parit, et nihil in universitate infecundum est."
       Quoted in Ivan Illich, *In the Vineyard of the Text. A Commentary to Hugh's
       Didascalicon* (Chicago: University of Chicago Press, 1993), p. 123.

Purple Sailor

Never have they seen such a thing
as this Sea-Gelly.
It drifts on the open sea,
a concussion of light,
at peace by the thousands.

E.M. Beekman

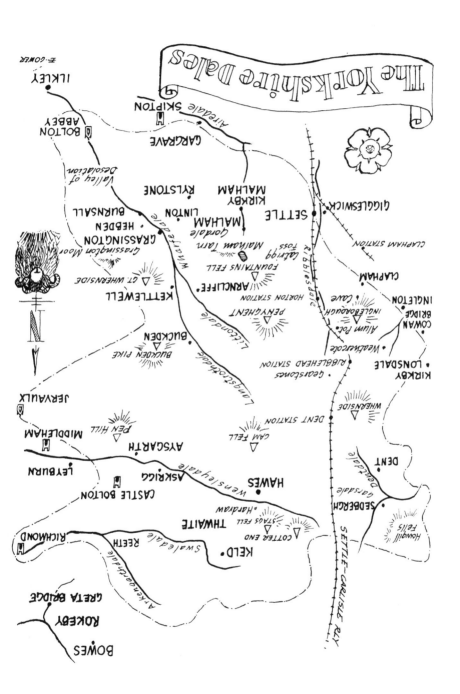

The Yorkshire Dales

A Yorkshire
Dales Anthology